DMS
3-05
FoL
18.95

Vietnamese AMERICANS

Our Cultural Heritage

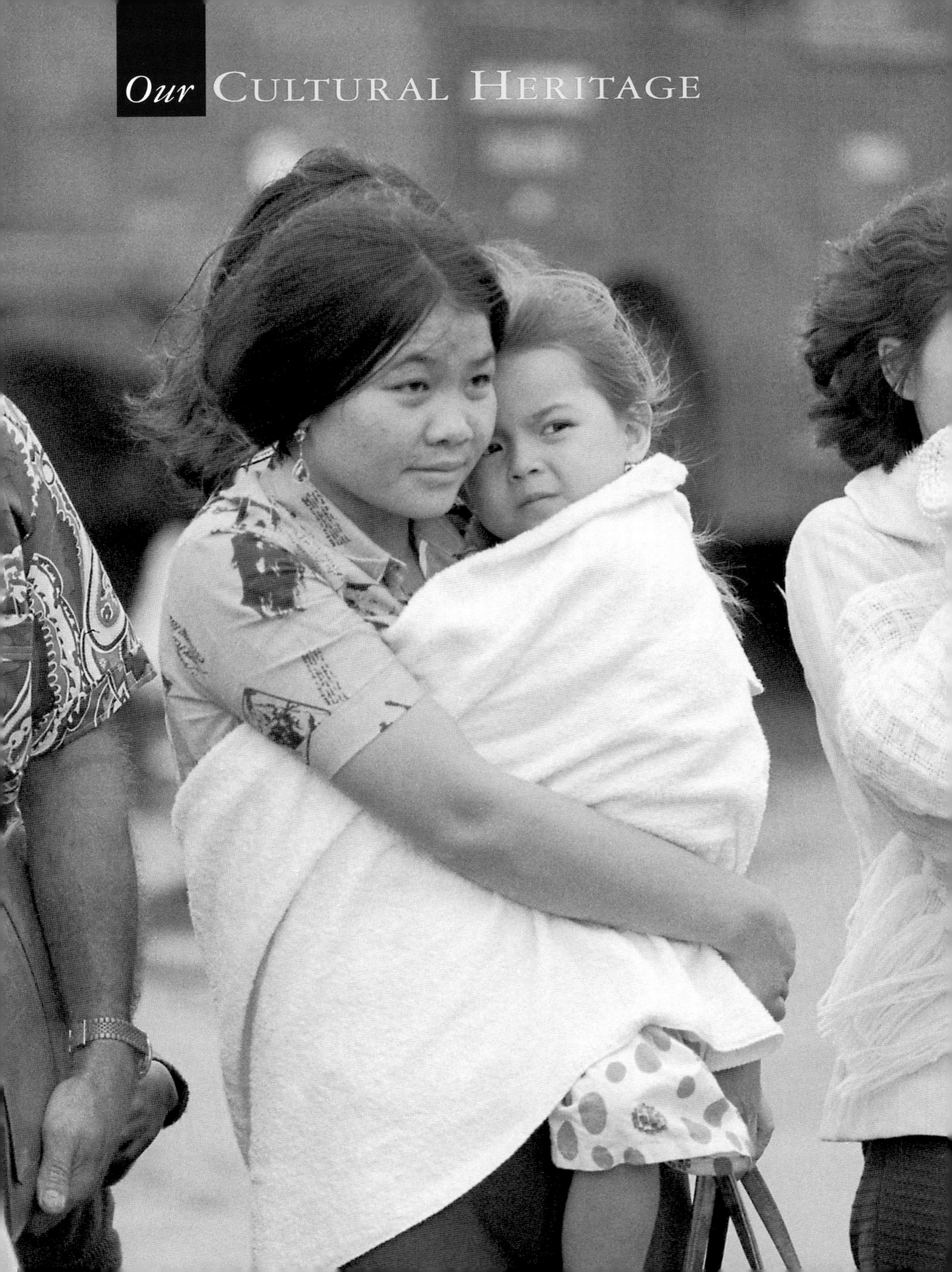

SPIRIT
of America®

Vietnamese AMERICANS

By C. Ann Fitterer

The Child's World®
Chanhassen, Minnesota

7

Vietnamese AMERICANS

Published in the United States of America by The Child's World®
PO Box 326 • Chanhassen, MN 55317-0326 • 800-599-READ • www.childsworld.com

Acknowledgments
The Child's World®: Mary Berendes, Publishing Director

Editorial Directions, Inc.: E. Russell Primm, Emily Dolbear, Sarah E. De Capua, and Lucia Raatma, Editors;
Linda S. Koutris, Photo Selector; Image Select International, Photo Research; Red Line Editorial and Pam
Rosenberg, Fact Research; Tim Griffin/IndexServ, Indexer; Chad Rubel, Proofreader

Photos
Cover/frontispiece: A Vietnamese-American refugee holding her small child after arriving in Arkansas in 1975

Cover photographs ©: Corbis/Bettmann; Catherine Karnow/Corbis

Interior photographs ©: Corbis, 6; TRIP/B.Vikander, 7; NARA, 8 top; Getty Images, 8 bottom, 9, 10, 11
top; Corbis, 11 bottom, 12, 13; GAMMA, 14; Corbis, 15, 16, TRIP/G. Stokoe; Getty Images/Eyewire, 18
top; TRIP/T.Freeman, 18 bottom; TRIP/S.Grant, 19; Corbis, 20, 21; TRIP/S.Grant, 23 top, 23 bottom;
Topham/ImageWorks, 24; Corbis, 25, 26; Topham/ImageWorks, 27; Corbis, 28 top, 28 bottom.

Library of Congress Cataloging-in-Publication Data
Fitterer, C. Ann.
  Vietnamese Americans / by C. Ann Fitterer.
     p. cm.
Includes index.
Summary: Brief introduction to Vietnamese Americans, their historical
backgrounds, customs, and traditions, their impact on society, and life
in the United States today.
1. Vietnamese Americans—Juvenile literature. 2. Refugees—United
States—Juvenile literature. [1. Vietnamese Americans. 2. Refugees.] I. Title.
  E184.V53 F58 2003
  305.895'92073—dc21
                              2001007388

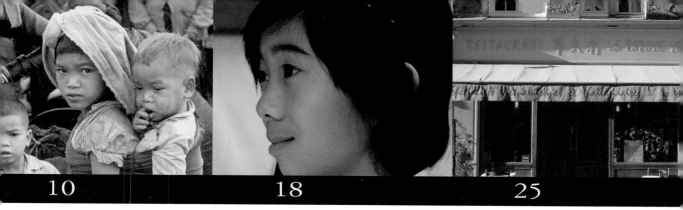

10   18   25

Contents

Chapter ONE

Escaping a Country of War

A Vietnamese-American family in Virginia during the 1990s

THE AMERICAN PEOPLE REPRESENT PEOPLE from countries all over the world. Many Americans have ancestors—family members from past generations—who arrived in the United States hundreds of years ago. And many of those ancestors came 100 years ago. Some Americans, however, have not been in America that long.

Americans from Vietnamese families are among the groups who recently arrived in America. Most Vietnamese Americans have come here since the 1970s. They came from a country destroyed by war.

At that time, Vietnam was divided into two countries.

One country was known as North Vietnam; the other was South Vietnam. In North Vietnam, the government was **communist**.

The countryside of Vietnam, a warm, mostly rural country

South Vietnam did not believe in the communist form of government, however. So the two countries went to war.

The Vietnam War began in 1957. Finally, North Vietnam took control of the government of South Vietnam. The South Vietnamese people were then forced to accept communism. Leaders of the old government were put in prison, along with people who did not agree with the new government or its way of life. The people had almost no freedom and they became very afraid.

During the war, much of Vietnam's land had been ruined. Farmland was destroyed. Farmers had to flee to safety. As a result, few farms were left after the war ended. So the people of Vietnam did not have enough food.

Interesting Fact

▶ Vietnam is in Asia, south of China. It is about the size of the state of New Mexico, but it is long and narrow.

7

Vietnamese refugees leaving their country after the war

Refugees often crowded onto small boats for their trip to a new country.

They grew even more worried and afraid.

Many Vietnamese wanted to move to a different country. But the communist government would not let them leave. People started to make their own plans to escape from Vietnam. Some people took many years to complete their escape plans. They had to save money. Some people had to change their jobs. Some jobs, like fishing, provided more opportunity for escape. The people who escaped Vietnam were called **refugees**.

Most people escaped from Vietnam by boat. Refugees crowded onto small fishing boats and sailed to nearby countries. The sea voyage was very dangerous. The boats were small and usually carried

8

many more people than they were designed for. In addition, boats could **capsize** easily in rough waters.

Some people died of starvation on the boats. They had little food to bring and no room to store it. They often ran out of fresh water long before the boat landed.

An American ship carrying Vietnamese refugees into Philippine waters

Another danger was sea pirates. These were men who attacked the refugee boats. The sea pirates took all the refugees' money. Then they captured or

killed the refugees. They would often steal the boat and take it with them.

Many refugees who left Vietnam never made it to another country. It is estimated that half of the refugees who left Vietnam died. Hundreds of thousands escaped, though. They arrived in the countries of Malaysia, Thailand, China, the Philippines, or Indonesia.

Chapter TWO

Struggles to Find a New Home

Once in a new country, Vietnamese families had to find jobs and places to live.

AFTER ARRIVING SAFELY IN ANOTHER COUNTRY, the Vietnamese refugees faced the beginning of the many struggles they would have to overcome. Some countries would not accept them. Then they had to travel to yet another country, hoping for safety.

When they *were* allowed to enter a country, there was nowhere for the refugees to live. They were not citizens of the country. They had no jobs, no money,

10

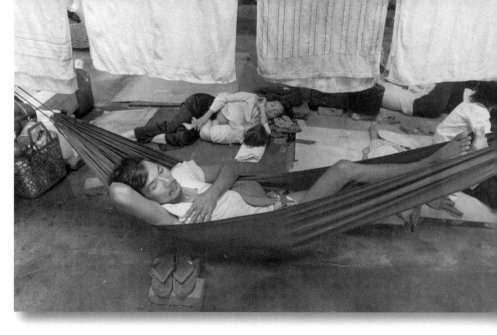

and no belongings. Governments of some of the countries placed them in refugee camps.

Life in a refugee camp was a daily struggle. There was no running water and very little food. Usually, there were no buildings. People often made shelters of branches and leaves. They slept on the ground. There were no activities and the days were endless. Often, refugees moved from one camp to another. Many Vietnamese refugees lived in these camps for a year or more before they were able to leave for a permanent home.

America was one of the countries where Vietnamese refugees hoped to live. They had heard of the freedom that Americans in the United States

Living in a refugee camp (above) could be hard, but certain groups tried to provide food (below) for the refugees.

A Vietnamese-American couple in front of their Pittsburgh apartment

enjoyed. They knew there were jobs for them in America. They knew there was housing, too, and plenty of food.

Various groups and organizations in the United States served as **sponsors** for Vietnamese refugees. These groups sent planes to carry the refugees to the United States. Often, the organizations helped the refugees when they arrived. Many of these organizations were religious groups and churches.

Two waves of Vietnamese refugees came to the United States. The first group of 125,000 people came right after the war in Vietnam ended in 1975. The second wave came a few years later. These people were Vietnamese who had stayed in their country and lived under the communist government.

This group of refugees arrived in the United States between 1979 and 1982. Many of these refugees came to join family members who had already escaped and had settled in the United States.

Another group of these later Vietnamese were the children of American soldiers. The United States sent soldiers to fight in the Vietnam War. While they were there, many soldiers fathered children. These children and their Vietnamese mothers and other family members were allowed to come to the United States.

Many children who came to America after the war had Vietnamese mothers and American fathers.

W HEN THE REFUGEES FROM VIETNAM ARRIVED IN THE UNITED STATES, they went to several different states. Many of the refugees arrived in California. One popular destination was southern California, in Orange County. This area became known as Little Saigon. Saigon was the capital of South Vietnam, which was renamed Ho Chi Minh City in 1975.

The people living in Little Saigon enjoyed one another's company. They found it easier to keep their Vietnamese traditions alive. The

climate was also hot, much like the climate in Vietnam.

Over the years, many Vietnamese Americans who lived in other American cities have moved to the "Little Saigon" area in Orange County, California. There are thousands of successful Vietnamese businesses, services, and organizations there.

Malls carry traditional Vietnamese clothing. Fast-food shops feature Vietnamese dishes. Bookstores sell newspapers and books in Vietnamese. There are places of worship for those of the Catholic or Buddhist faith. Places for sports and recreation feature traditional Vietnamese games such as *co tuaong*, which is a Chinese form of chess, as well as Western games, such as soccer or pool.

Chapter THREE

New Struggles in a New Land

AFTER ARRIVING IN THE UNITED STATES, MANY struggles were over for the refugees. They were safe now. They did not have to worry about surviving the refugee camps. But they had to face many new problems.

It was often difficult to find housing, for example. The Vietnamese did not have jobs. It was hard to pay for a place to live. Many Vietnamese people had lived in **rural** areas of Vietnam. They had farmed and fished for a living. They had no idea what life was like in a big city, but many of them were brought to cities to live anyway. In Vietnam,

A street in the Little Saigon section of Los Angeles

the climate is hot and **humid**. There is no snow. But many refugees were brought to live in places where it gets very cold. It was a hard adjustment for them.

A temple in the Vietnam city of Hanoi

Language was also a major **obstacle**. The Vietnamese refugees did not know English, and it was a difficult language for them to learn. In Vietnamese, words are very short, usually just one **syllable**. But many English words have more than one syllable. This was hard to get used to.

Although many Vietnamese people were Catholic, most of them were Buddhist when they came to the United States. The Vietnamese

Vietnamese food consists mostly of rice, fish, and vegetables.

Vietnamese children had to adjust to American schools.

Buddhists found fewer temples for worship in America than there are in Vietnam.

In Vietnam, people ate mostly rice, fish, and vegetables. However, the food was prepared differently from the way food was prepared in the United States. Over time, they learned where to find the ingredients they needed to prepare the foods as they wished.

Children found school in the United States was a difficult adjustment, too. They were not used to the many books and materials students had in American schools. The hardest thing was doing what the American teachers expected of them. In Vietnam, students were expected to memorize material that the teacher assigned. They did not ask questions. They did not show curiosity. But the

American teachers expected them to ask questions! They were expected to be curious and do research to find answers to things they wanted to know.

Some Vietnamese Americans were victims of **discrimination**, too. Some Americans did not want Vietnamese people in the United States. They were afraid the Vietnamese might take jobs away from other Americans who had lived in the country longer.

Despite all of their struggles to adjust to life in the United States, the Vietnamese did not give up. They had survived many difficulties in their journey to America. They were determined to succeed. And they were happy to be in America. They knew that hard work was the key to success in their new country.

A Vietnamese-American police officer

The most important Vietnamese holiday of the year is called Tet. This is the Vietnamese New Year. It takes place in February and is celebrated for three days with many major celebrations. Tet begins with fireworks on the evening before the first day. Families have a special celebration in their homes. This is a time to be with friends and relatives.

Tet is also a colorful celebration. People dress in brightly colored clothing during the three days. They serve brightly colored foods, too. One special food served for Tet is called *bahn Tet*. These are rice cakes made with beans, pepper, and pork. This mixture is wrapped in banana leaves that make the cakes bright green.

20

A common event of a Tet festival is a dragon dance (opposite). The dragon has special meaning for the Vietnamese people, so it has a special place at the festival. People at the festivals are there to have fun and enjoy themselves. There are also contests and booths that sell different things.

Small temples also have an important role in Tet festivals. People at the festivals go into the temples and pray for peace (below). They also pray for the relatives they left behind in Vietnam. And they honor and remember their Vietnamese ancestors who are no longer alive.

Chapter FOUR

Vietnamese Americans in the 21st Century

HUNDREDS OF THOUSANDS OF VIETNAMESE Americans have lived in the United States for more than 25 years. But in those 25 years, they have found ways to be successful individually and as a cultural group.

Many organizations and groups have been formed by Vietnamese Americans. These groups assist people of the Vietnamese **culture** to find success, to continue their culture, and to find happiness in the United States. They provide Vietnamese Americans with

A Vietnamese-American youth group in Huntington Beach, California

opportunities to socialize and celebrate holidays together.

Today, America has many strong Vietnamese Catholic and Buddhist groups as well as Vietnamese Lions Service Clubs and Boy Scout troops. Some groups are dedicated to the education of Vietnamese Americans. They may offer scholarships or professional training programs.

In the past 25 years, many Vietnamese Americans have left towns and cities in the colder areas of the United States for warmer cities with more established Vietnamese communities.

Some Vietnamese students continue to struggle in school because of differences in language and culture. However, a large number of Vietnamese students are among the top students in their classes. Young adult Vietnamese Americans are finding success in education, business, and professional positions such as lawyers and doctors.

Vietnamese Americans have formed their own neighborhoods (above) and taken jobs in various fields, such as teaching (below).

23

Many Vietnamese-American children have taken up all-American sports like baseball.

Vietnamese-American children enjoy the American way of life. Like other American children, they spend their time riding bikes, in-line skating, playing football, and listening to popular music. Many speak English more fluently than Vietnamese—the language that is often still spoken in their homes.

It is not always easy for families, though, when the children **adapt** so quickly. Sometimes this causes problems in Vietnamese-American families. In the Vietnamese culture, children obey their parents without asking questions. They have few choices. But this can be hard for Vietnamese-American children when they see the freedom and choices that other American children have.

The arrival of Vietnamese people in America has added another set of foods, arts, and traditions to the United States. The Viet-

Vietnamese restaurants can be found throughout the United States.

namese people share their music with audiences across America. Vietnamese restaurants are now a common sight in American cities. Cooking in the traditional Vietnamese way is easy today for Vietnamese Americans. Many stores specialize in the utensils and ingredients needed for this style of cooking.

The Vietnamese have had another important impact on life in the United States. Many towns in America relied on people in the fishing industry. Slowly, this line of work quit attracting people. People

Showing respect is very important in the Vietnamese culture, and customs can be surprising. For example, it is considered disrespectful to look someone in the eye.

The skills of Vietnamese fishermen are appreciated in the United States.

moved out of the towns looking for different work. But many Vietnamese people had been fishermen before coming to the United States. They moved to some of these fishing towns and began to fish in the nearby waters. Their hard work and dedication has revived many of these towns and villages, and they are successful fishing areas once again.

Moving to the United States was—and continues to be—filled with difficult struggles for Vietnamese Americans. But their courage,

hard work, family values, and commitment to education have helped them find ways to be successful in a culture very different from their homeland. Their time in America has been very short compared to the other groups of people whose ancestors came to the United States from faraway countries. But as they have for the past 25 years, Vietnamese Americans will continue to add to the American way of life and make the American culture even richer.

Vietnamese Americans are succeeding in the United States because of education, hard work, and courage.

Vietnamese Foods

THE TRADITIONAL VIETNAMESE MEAL CONSISTS of rice, fresh vegetables, and fish. Much of Vietnam borders the sea, so fresh fish and seafood are always available. Vietnamese Americans continue to enjoy fish and seafood. When they eat meat, they often prefer pork. The Vietnamese also enjoy many fruits.

One type of Vietnamese soup (right), called *Cahh bi Dao*, is made of pork, squash, and onions. A common sauce with Vietnamese food is made from anchovies, a type of fish, and salt. It is mixed with garlic, water, sugar, lemon juice, and chili pepper. This is called *nuoc Cham*. This spicy sauce is used like many Americans use ketchup!

Tea is a favorite Vietnamese beverage (below). While some Americans drink tea with milk, sugar, honey, or lemon, many Vietnamese add dried flowers.

The Vietnamese do not eat sweets the way many Americans do. Another American habit that was new to the Vietnamese was eating greasy fried foods.

Most Vietnamese Americans have added some American foods to their diet. But few have given up the traditional Vietnamese ways of cooking and seasoning their foods. Instead, they are sharing these dishes with other Americans. Americans have adopted many Vietnamese foods and are enjoying them in thousands of successful Vietnamese restaurants all over the United States.

Time LINE

939

1975

2000s

208 B.C A tribe from southern China called the *Viets* settles in the northern region of what is now Vietnam.

939 The Vietnamese overthrow Chinese rule in their country and establish independence that will last for 900 years.

1535 The Portuguese are the first Europeans to enter Vietnam in their search for new trade routes throughout Southeast Asia.

Early 1800s The French enter Vietnam to find it split into three separate sections. Over the next 80 years, the French will bring these parts together to create a unified Vietnam.

1883–1945 The French colonize and rule Vietnam.

1945 Vietnamese leader Ho Chi Minh breaks from French rule and establishes the independent Democratic Republic of Vietnam. Conflict between this group and France continues for some time.

1954 Vietnam is divided into North Vietnam and South Vietnam.

1957 Conflicts increase between communist and noncommunist groups.

1965 The United States becomes involved in the Vietnam War.

1975 The Vietnam War ends. Vietnam becomes one communist country. The first wave of Vietnamese refugees arrives in the United States.

1979 The second wave of Vietnamese refugees begins to arrive in the U.S.

1982 The number of Vietnamese refugees allowed into the United States drops and continues to remain low for the following eight years.

1983 The U.S. government establishes the Orderly Departure Program, a program that allows Vietnamese to enter the United States as immigrants seeking citizenship. Many families and friends are finally reunited.

1985 Jean Nguyen and Hung Vu become the first Vietnamese Americans to graduate from the U.S. Military Academy at West Point.

1990 The Vietnamese Fishermen's Association wins an important court case that grants Vietnamese living in the United States but who are not citizens the right to do commercial fishing off the California coast.

1991 The 1990 U.S. census shows that the Vietnamese are the third largest Asian-American group in the nation.

adapt (uh-DAPT)
To adapt is to change something to suit a new situation. Many Vietnamese-American children adapt more quickly than their parents to life in the United States.

capsize (kap-SYZ)
To capsize means to turn over in the water. Vietnamese refugee boats often capsized in rough waters.

communist (KOM-yuh-nihst)
A communist country follows the beliefs of communism, a political system in which the government owns everything. Vietnam has a communist government.

culture (KUHL-chuhr)
A culture is the way of life, ideas, customs, and traditions of a group of people. The culture of Vietnam is much different from the culture of the United States, but Vietnamese Americans have blended the cultures together.

discrimination (dihs-krim-ih-NAY-shuhn)
Discrimination is unjust behavior toward others based on differences in age, race, gender, or other factors. Many Vietnamese Americans have faced discrimination in the United States.

humid (HYOO-mid)
Humid means damp and moist. The climate in Vietnam is very humid.

obstacle (OB-stuh-kuhl)
An obstacle is something that gets in your way or prevents you from doing something. The English language was an obstacle for Vietnamese Americans.

refugees (ref-yuh-JEEZ)
Refugees are people who are forced to leave their homes because of war, persecution, or a natural disaster. The people who left Vietnam after the war were refugees.

rural (ROOR-uhl)
The word rural is used to describe the countryside or farming. Most people in Vietnam lived in rural areas, so they found U.S. cities to be strange places.

sponsors (SPON-suhrz)
A sponsor gives people money and other kinds of support. Many U.S. groups served as sponsors for Vietnamese refugees.

syllable (SIL-uh-buhl)
A syllable is a unit of sound in a word. A syllable contains a vowel and possibly one or more consonants. The word *long* contains only one syllable. Most words in the Vietnamese language are made of just one syllable.

Internet Sites

Visit our homepage for lots of links about Vietnamese Americans:
http://www.childsworld.com/links.html

Note to Parents, Teachers, and Librarians:
We routinely verify our Web links to make sure they're safe,
active sites—so encourage your readers to check them out!

Books

Hoyt-Goldsmith, Diane. *Hoang Ang: A Vietnamese-American Boy.* New York: Holiday House, 1992.

McKay, Lawrence. *Journey Home.* New York: Lee & Low Books, 2000.

O'Connor, Karen. *Dan Thuy's New Life in America.* Minneapolis: Lerner Publications, 1992.

Scoones, Simon. *A Family from Vietnam.* Austin, Tex.: Raintree/Steck-Vaughn, 1998.

Springstubb, Tricia. *The Vietnamese-Americans.* San Diego: Lucent Books, 2001.

Places to Visit or Contact

Vietnamese American Cultural and Social Council
611 North 13th Street
San Jose, CA 95112
408-971-8280

Vietnamese American Society
P.O. Box 50371
Washington, DC 20091

The Wing Luke Asian Museum
407 Seventh Avenue South
Seattle, WA 98104
206-623-5124

Index